C. Churchill

Screaming into the Forest

Collected Poems

C. Churchill

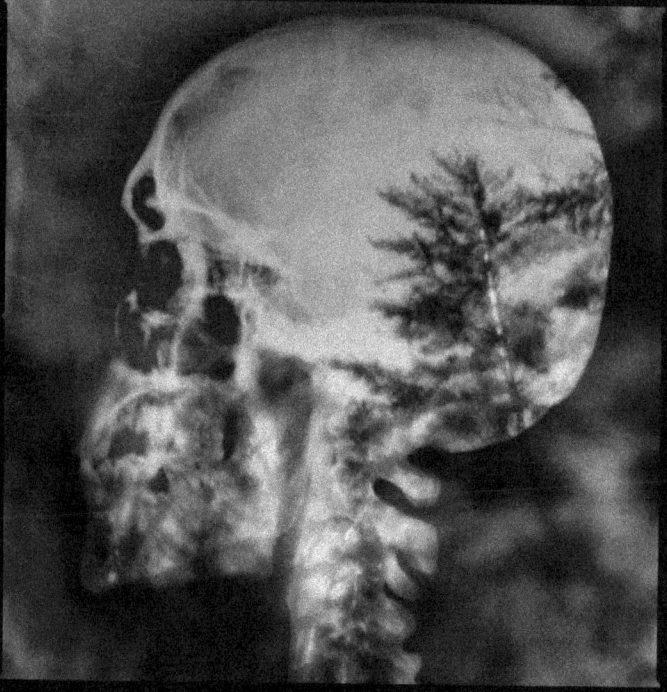

SCREAMING INTO THE FOREST

lungs filled with confusion
letting go of illusion
we scream

Screaming into the Forest

other books available by C. Churchill
Petals of the Moon
Wildflower Tea
Ravens Moon
Mirror Mirror
Chasing Pines
Racing Ravens

on social media @cc_writes

Dedicated to those who find themselves a little lost and
a little misplaced but are still here
to scream another day.

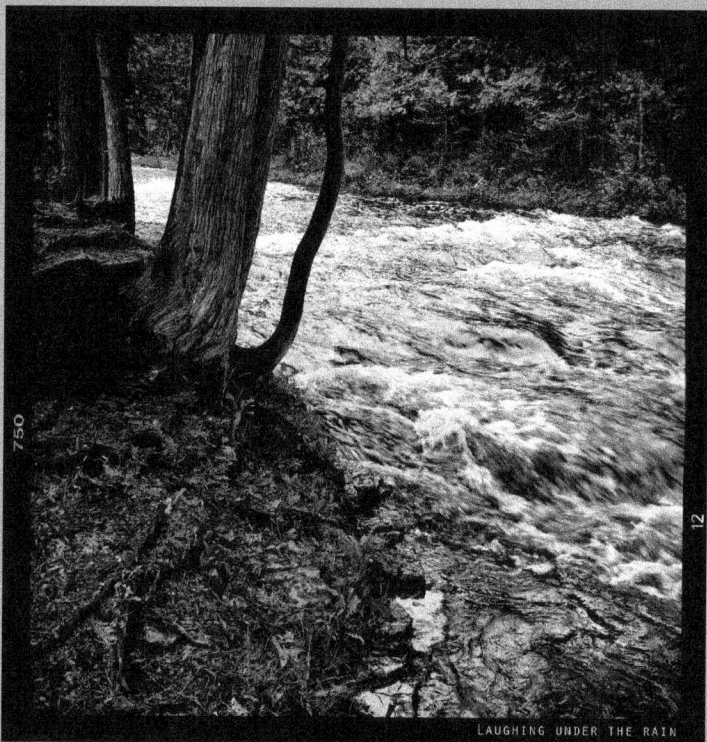

750

12

LAUGHING UNDER THE RAIN

Screaming into the forest
laughing under the rain
trying everything I can
to beat this pace

the pace of breaking
the pace of pain
where I was left on the edge
laughing under the rain

but we have all been there
in one way or another
screaming into a void
running for cover

a breath a light
a sense of new
the pace comes to calm
inside of you

A smallish hand rests in mine
we can't even decide on day or time
for what is too short
or what is too long
when hands fill spaces
that go beyond

750

12

To Be Alive

littered in have nots,
cannots and
forget me nots

we strive
to be alive
in a field of forgotten promises

we strive
for baby's breath among sunflowers death
to be alive

we feed on seed and attempt to grow
but what of the no show
what of the have nots

we still strive
to be alive

DECISIONS

in longing for normalcy
I have found complacency
a new way to cope
a new way to dream
in a world without a compass
a new way to scream

in a world full of new
the choices are endless
and some days I feel lost
some days feel relentless
but at the end of it all
the stars still show me the way
compass or not I am here today

places we go
to scream
to let it go
to let ourselves crumble
those are the places
we can truly call home

walk into the wild
take your place
in the unknown
litter you path with blooms
so, they know you
have grown

750

12

CHARMED

I spent some time bleeding
wondering if this was my death
wondering if anyone would notice
I had become lifeless

but alas the sun charmed me this morning
and the moon sang me a song a few nights past
and the forest holds my soul
not ready for me to pass

The slightest wind
causes a ripple
the ripple changes
to waves

the sparkle from
the daylight
changes to smiles
and my heart fills
as tears spill
in the slightest wind

KALEIDOSCOPE

I collect my pieces
after the breaking
they never fit quite the same
but they are mine
and in the mirror
I have learned to enjoy
a kaleidoscope of me

750   '23   FEATHERS

Feathers dark
overhead they call

a moment flashes
before my fall

to fly, a dream
to see beyond

under these clouds
we thrive upon

under these lids
in darkness free

the feathers hark
in this rhapsody

750

NEEDLES

needles lay soft
on the forest floor

a feeling lost
nothing more

only a gasp
at the occasional poke

on my flesh
a blood let soak

reminding me
of my breath

and that it is necessary
to take this rest

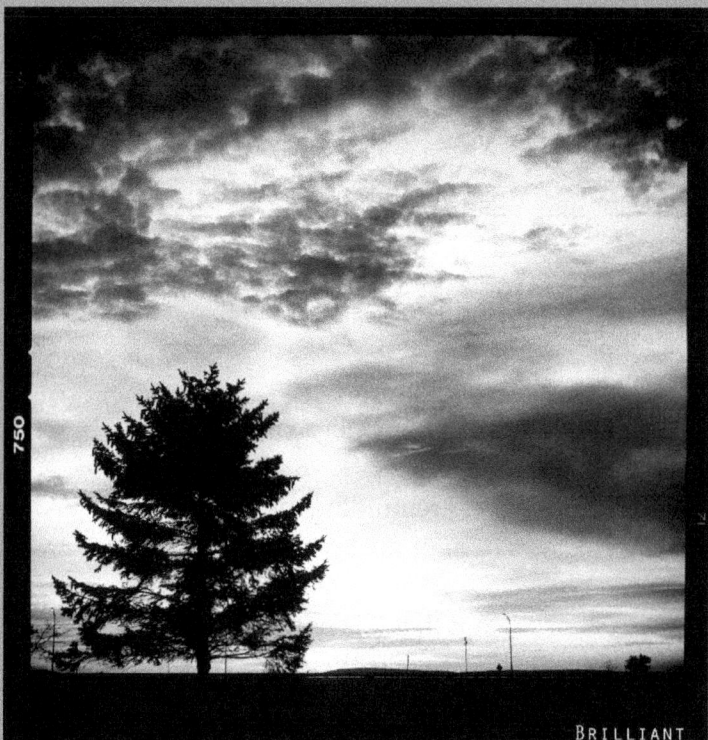

walk with me
into a different time
I will show you my brilliant side
the one when I still cared
when I still shared
before the dust covered my soul
before I was let down
grouped into the old
put out to pasture
sent on my way
but I can tell you to this very day
I am still young, and I still share
I just reserve my brilliance for those who care

750

12

PETALS

I let the petals fall like rain
onto my flesh
freshly lain

covering my scars
reflecting in stars
eyes and thighs and all the lies

I let the petals fall like rain
grasping at the beauty
in lieu of the pain

SHADOWS

love is here
in shadows stark
just a hop and leap
over from my heart

love is here
it has never left
it pours like rain
in every breath

love is here
and it will remain
no matter the darkness
no matter
the rain

750

COVER ME

I have never lived for them
I have never grown for them

but the trees still call me
and I answer

in mutual magic
in mutual respect

They allow me to scream
and I allow them to cover me

dazzle me with the stars in your eyes
not your litany of lies

I never needed you to impress
just to try
if anything,
your half best

instead, you colored
your gray away
and all I could see was
someone else's day

a truth that did not belong
in the eyes that once said home

750

CREATION

sunlight graces me
in contemplation

and I answer in
creation

PLUNDER

your hand to my breast
replies in a smile
that screams success
but all the while

my heart is under
fathoms deep
too far to plunder
to be in your keep

NOT FOR ANYONE

I rip them off
like bandages
these tears that cut me

I shove the thread ends
into my smile
as I limp through each stitch

broken as the come
but I won't lay down
not for them, not for anyone

fate smiles down
as if it knows

that my get up and go
has gotten up and left

but still, it smiles
making sense of it all

making me feel
that it is okay to fall

and fall I will
again, and again

for it is how we grow
and how we win

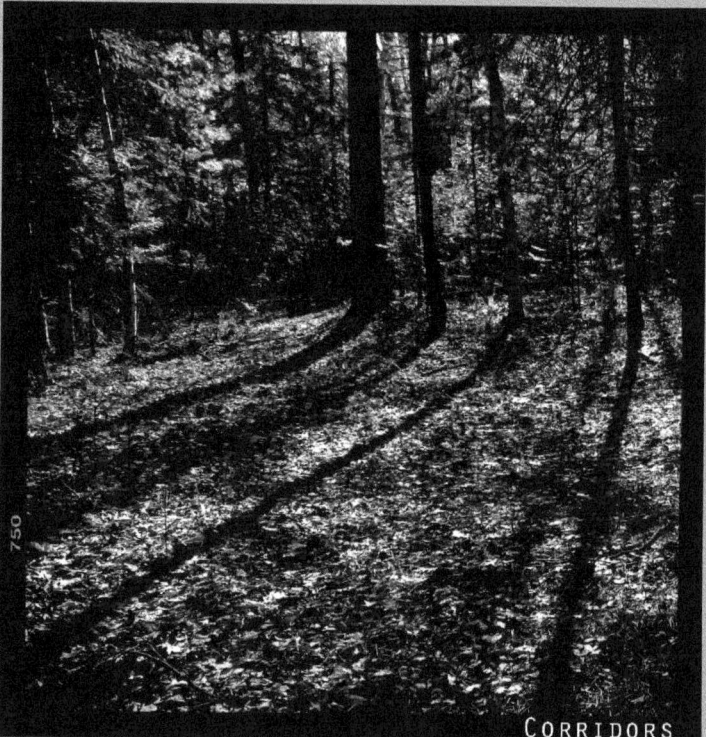

750

CORRIDORS

we walk into darkness
not knowing the way
as we smooth our hands
along corridors and alter our steps

we walk in the darkness
full of light
and even if we slow our pace
we are assured
we know this place

bless this burden
laid upon my soul

bless this pain
making me strive for more

bless this heart
for it still beats

sometimes in hope
and sometimes in memories

WINTER

Shocking as the winter
a blanket of white warms
it steams in promises
of a new spring morn
curled up in smoke
sickly sweet streams
circling above
these cold winter dreams

You shook me to my core
nothing less
but wanting more
the wind rushed
taking every leaf
leaving no trace
of summers heat
but in these timbers
you still dwell
making a hearth
into a hell

I have walked on eggshells
I have broken glass
hot coals at the ready
knowing this too shall pass

but my mind still wanders
to thoughts of old
thoughts of you
and I grow cold

missing pieces
a puzzle destroyed

throw a tantrum
onto the floor

what a waste of time
and energy to boot

to have an incomplete picture
of what we assumed

but we still play
this game of chance

hoping to have
another first dance

iron birds
fall from grace
holding my throat
in its place

bars for wings
and heavy the feather
sure to drown
in any weather

yet they soar
rising new heights
keeping voices locked
and out of flight

750

12

SLITHER

slithering in the grass
awaiting a kill
you don't mind
you will get your fill

you slither, confident
self-assured
that your target ultimately
will be yours

breathing in all the light
throwing shade to those in plight
because the weak succumb
you know this to be true

as you continue to slither
nothing here is new

DAYS OF BLUE

watchful eyes
on rainy days
see the blur
memories they play

placing figures
in the rain
as moments you left
experiencing pain

a tear, a drop
a wetness new
but all too familiar
in days of blue

750

GRAB THE MOONLIGHT

pour it out
pour it on
pour and pour
half empty
half full
always pouring
till there is nothing more

refill
recharge
eat the sunshine
amidst the lies
grab the moonlight
inside these eyes

write and write and write
some more because
there is wealth in words
that feed the pour

BRUISED FRUIT

750

soften the vines
a strong embrace

bruised this fruit
out of place

rolled on concrete
a seed falls through

under darkness
it waits anew

750

SHEETS

my wars have turned history to scars
and memories to stars
but the outcome is hazy
as piles of casings shell at my feet
and I scream to be set free
from these lead sheets

a pause in fighting
a well-deserved rest
for a warrior that
has always tried their best

but alas here we are screaming
piling casings into a home
hoping the sheets are enough
to keep us warm

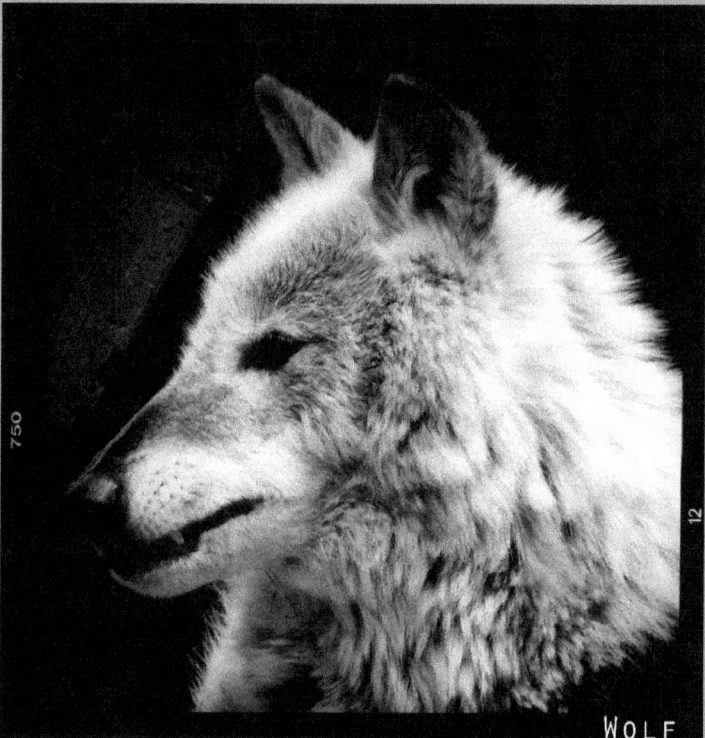

750

12

WOLF

fangs have ripped flesh
in all the right ways
where I still crave the wolf
to this very day

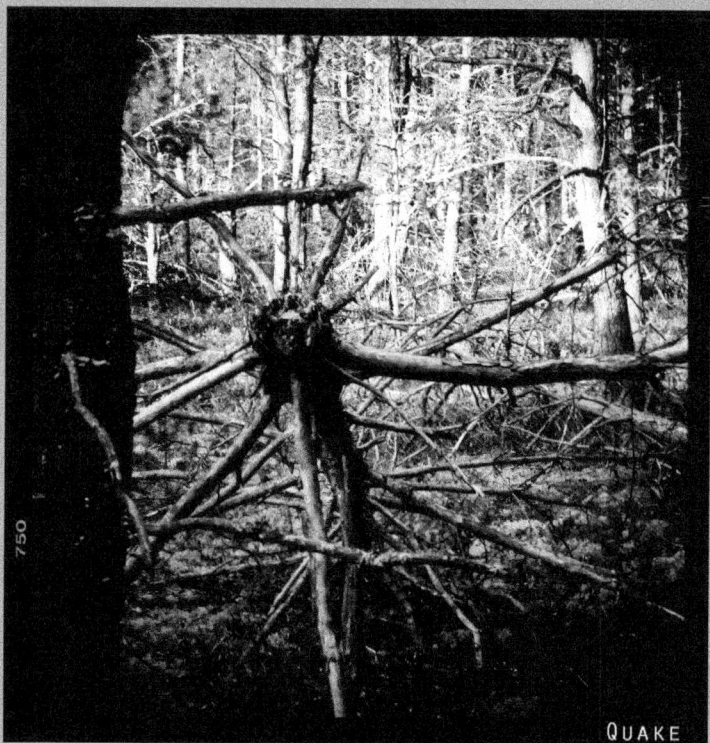

750

QUAKE

idle these hands
for they quake

in your proximity
I cannot still

my heart is afire
and my body responds

for a breath taken
is given back tenfold

and your arms
mold to mine

as if we are a liar
cursing love for lust

and giving breath freely
in a quaking trust

RIVALS

I dream of a love
that rivals
a silent snowfall

when a pin could drop
and still the only sound that you hear
is your heart beating wildly

THRIVE

lay me down
not six feet under
but six feet above
above expectations
its where I thrive
where I am alive
where I expect
not to land
but to fly

keep me close
I breathe in code

under sheets of silk
that whisper behold

secrets play on imagination
kisses are felt beyond inspiration

keep me close
I am worth the time

for whom else will paint a masterpiece
with you in mind

750

SURVIVOR

to the ends of the earth
my feet follow
the sun, the moon
and darkness between

through chill of night
and blazing deserts
I follow
leaving what I knew

forging through
that is what survivors do
just keep on
following their feet

and making anew
making it true

you will always
find blooms
in your valley of thorns

I heard you
from the other side

a voice behind
every tear I cried

your sweet songs
whisper on the leaves

an echo of your heart
in every breeze

by my side
as you said forever

our sweet love song
not even death can sever

750

⊕ 8

RELEASE

run fast
then faster

get to the cover
get to the trees

get to your voice
get to the scream

release the demons
release the pain

tell the darkness
it won't win today

750

MARSHMALLOWS

if my only sin
is protecting my heart
then send me to hell
with the bitch
you think I have become
we will roast marshmallows
on the flames
enjoying our truth

SUNSET TOWN

I grew up in a sunset town
where all life drips into ebony sheets
where time was lost in waves
where we danced on the moon
sleeping on the wake
we kissed our dreams into stars
and we called it home

I traced my future
across their skin
foretelling many years
of playful sin

watching their chest
rise then fall
my heart smiling
eyes revealing it all

my favorite secret
they had become
pulling me back
from being numb

I had fallen
caught in these arms
not even once
sounding an alarm

THE FOREST TRUE

I was born of limbs and boughs
under moonlit nights
and starry nows

born to bleed
and born to cry
born to live before I die

breath I have chosen
under a canopy of blue
an exchange of life in the forest true

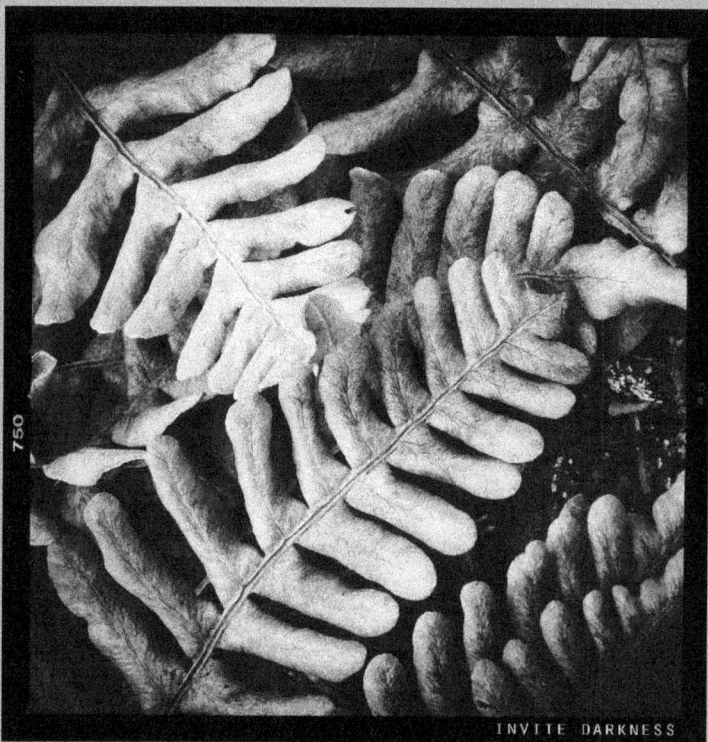
750

INVITE DARKNESS

I lie underneath these ferns
watching the sun play pleasantries
upon my skin
as shadows dance in juxtaposition
I realize
even in the light
I invite the darkness in

I feel the words
they dance on my heart

inking off my mind
bleeding into pages

on pulses they play
immortal they will stay

I feel the words
can you?

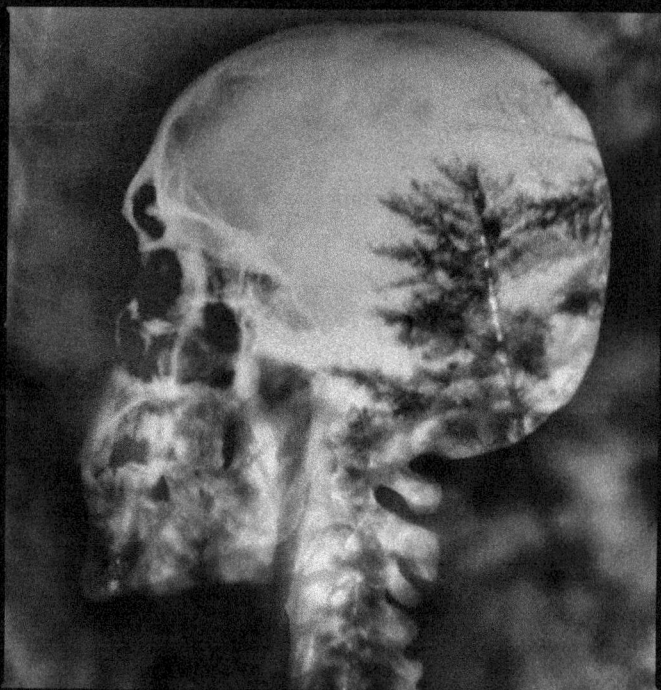

SCREAMING INTO THE FOREST

About the Author

C. Churchill currently resides in the forests of Northern Michigan. Writing and photographing nature and exploring the beauty of isolation.

Other books by C. Churchilll

Petals of the Moon
Wildflower Tea
Racing Ravens
Chasing Pines
Mirror Mirror
Ravens Moon

Laughing under the Rain will be available Spring 2022

Remember there is always a place to scream